THE OFFIC...
LIVERPOOL FC
ANNUAL
2006
Written by Paul Eaton

YOU'LL NEVER WALK ALONE

LIVERPOOL
FOOTBALL CLUB

EST·1892 ®

A Grange Publication

© 2005 Published by Grange Communications Ltd., Edinburgh.
Licensed by Granada Ventures Ltd. Printed in the EU.
© Photographs copyright Liverpool Football Club and Action Images

ISBN I 902704 90 8

£6.99

CONTENTS

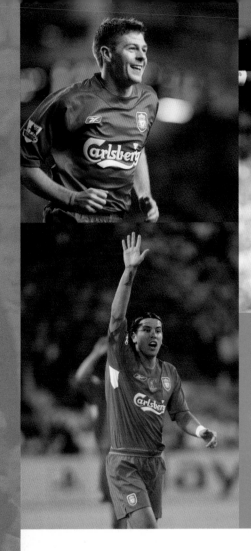

YOU'LL NEVER WALK ALONE

LIVERPOOL
FOOTBALL CLUB

EST·1892 ®

IAN CALLAGHAN HAS PLAYED MORE GAMES FOR LIVERPOO

The Reds were founded by John Houlding back in 1892.

LIVERPOOL
SEASON REVIEW: 2004-05

The 'Rafalution' began in earnest on a sunny Saturday afternoon in London as Rafael Benitez took charge of his first game as Liverpool manager away at Spurs. The Reds emerged with a creditable point after Djibril Cisse struck on his debut in a 1-1 draw.

AUGUST

The European campaign also got off to a good start as a Steven Gerrard double secured a 2-0 victory in Austria against AK Graz as the Reds put themselves in a great position to qualify for the group stages of the competition.

The first home game of the season brought the first three point return of the campaign as Manchester City were beaten 2-1 with goals from Milan Baros and Gerrard, who had now already netted three times after just three matches.

The end of the month finished disappointingly as Graz won 1-0 in the return at Anfield – although Liverpool progressed 2-1 on aggregate – and Bolton triumphed by a single goal at the Reebok Stadium as Benitez tasted Premiership defeat for the first time as Liverpool boss.

SEPTEMBER

Steven Gerrard was again on the scoresheet as the Reds cantered to a 3-0 victory over West Bromwich, with Steve Finnan and Luis Garcia netting their first goals of the campaign.

Liverpool made a fine start to their Champions League proper campaign, seeing off Monaco at Anfield with strikes from Djibril Cisse and Milan Baros, but delight turned to despair a few days later when Mikael Silvestre's double sent the Reds crashing to defeat at arch rivals Manchester United.

Promoted Norwich were on the receiving end of a Liverpool backlash the following weekend as the Reds ran out comfortable 3-0 winners, but the Champions League campaign took a turn for the worse when Rafa's men suffered a Greek tragedy in Athens, losing 1-0 to Olympiacos.

October started disappointingly for the Reds as Joe Cole's late strike gave Chelsea a

OCTOBER

slender victory at Stamford Bridge but, after an international break, Liverpool returned to form at Fulham and overturned a two goal half time deficit to run out 4-2 winners, with Igor Biscan among the scorers.

More Champions League disappointment followed as Spanish outfit Deportivo La Coruna held the Reds to a frustrating goalless draw at Anfield. With only four points collected from a possible nine at the halfway stage of the group campaign, qualification was looking difficult for Liverpool.

After Charlton were beaten 2-0 at Anfield the Reds then overcame their first hurdle in the Carling Cup as a young team ran out easy winners at Millwall.

Blackburn then took a point off Liverpool in an exciting 2-2 draw at Ewood Park, ensuring the Reds' disappointing early season record away from Anfield continued in Lancashire. It was a night to forget for Djibril Cisse who broke his leg in two places following an awkward fall and was told he wouldn't play again this season.

NOVEMBER

It was a 'must win' match as Liverpool went to Spain to face Deportivo La Coruna in Rafael Benitez's home country. Nothing less than a victory would be good enough to keep our qualification dreams alive, and the players produced the goods with a professional display which was rewarded with a 1-0 victory.

However, the league form continued to be inconsistent as Birmingham secured one of the shock results of the season with a 1-0 win at Anfield with a late strike from Darren Anderton.

Two victories followed in quick succession against Middlesbrough in the Carling Cup and Crystal Palace in the Premiership (Milan Baros hat-trick) before 'Boro exacted some revenge for their Cup defeat with a 2-0 win in the league at the Riverside Stadium.

When Liverpool then went and lost to a single goal in Monaco it meant we needed to beat Olympiacos at Anfield by two clear goals in our final group match to qualify for the knock-out stages.

Despite a frustrating month, the Reds ended on a high as Neil Mellor blasted home a last minute winner to seal a brilliant 2-1 victory over champions Arsenal.

DECEMBER

December started gloriously for the Reds who won a thrilling penalty shoot-out at Tottenham to move into the semi-finals of the Carling Cup. It was a real 'coming of age' night as the Liverpool youngsters showed there is life under the first team with a gutsy performance to see off their more experienced opponents.

After a 1-1 draw at Villa Park, where Harry Kewell opened his account for the

THE FINAL PLAYER TO SCORE IN FRONT O

season, all eyes were turned to Anfield as the Reds searched for a margin of victory over Olympiacos which would be good enough to take them into the last 16 of the Champions League.

When Rivaldo opened the scoring for the Greeks it looked like mission impossible for Liverpool, but after a second half display which will live long in the memories of Kopites all over the world, the Reds miraculously turned the game around as goals from Florent Sinama-Pongolle, Neil Mellor and Steven Gerrard almost took the roof off Anfield.

Again, though, delight was followed by despair just a few days later as Everton won the derby at Goodison while more league points slipped away in a 1-1 draw with Portsmouth at Anfield.

Three straight wins followed against Newcastle, West Bromwich and Southampton as the Reds enjoyed a happy Christmas and moved into 2005 well placed in all competitions.

The new year kicked off in the worst possible way as Liverpool suffered a

JANUARY

double blow, losing 1-0 to leaders Chelsea at Anfield and losing Xabi Alonso with a broken ankle which was to rule him out of action for three months.

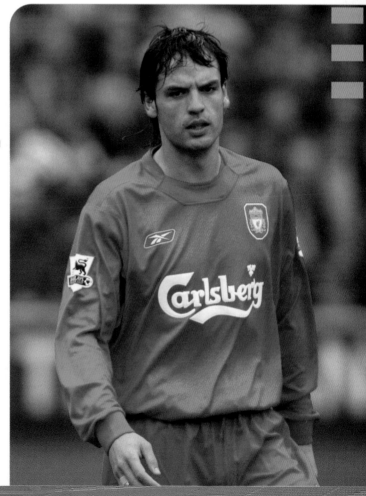

That bad news was tempered by the fact that Liverpool went quickly into the transfer market as soon as the window reopened, swooping for Real Madrid striker Fernando Morientes, defender Mauricio Pellegrino from Valencia and young goalkeeper Scott Carson who arrived from Leeds United.

After our scheduled FA Cup third round tie with Burnley was postponed because of a waterlogged pitch, the Reds turned their attentions to the Carling Cup semi-final with Watford and came through the first leg at Anfield with a 1-0 victory behind them thanks to Steven Gerrard's strike.

Southampton then sent Liverpool crashing to another away league defeat before they booked their place in the Carling Cup final with a 1-0 victory at Vicarage Road, sealing a 2-0 aggregate success over Watford.

But the FA Cup campaign lasted just one game as Djimi Traore's own goal saw the Reds on the receiving end of a Cup upset at Turf Moor.

February was another month of contrasting

FEBRUARY

fortunes for Rafael Benitez as he watched his side win and lose in the Premiership, progress in the Champions League but lose out in heartbreaking fashion in the Carling Cup final.

It started so well for the Reds as victories over both Charlton and Fulham in the Premiership kept them in touch with fourth placed Everton, but a poor performance at Birmingham resulted in a disappointing 2-0 defeat and a loss of momentum.

German side Bayer Leverkusen were our next opponents in the Champions League and arrived at Anfield for the last 16 clash having qualified from a group containing Real Madrid and Roma. If a difficult task faced the Reds then it never showed as goals from Luis Garcia, John Arne Riise and Didi Hamann gave us what appeared to be an unassailable 3-0 lead, before a late slip from Jerzy Dudek gifted the Germans an undeserved lifeline in the tie ahead of the second leg.

All roads then led to Wales for Liverpool fans as they embarked on yet another journey to the Millennium

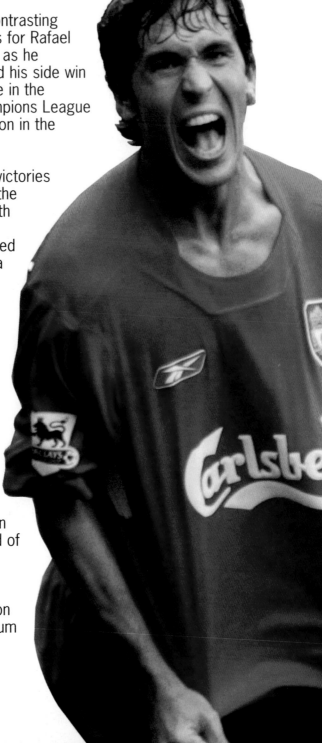

Stadium for the Carling Cup final against Chelsea.

John Arne Riise opened the scoring inside the first minute to give the Reds a dream start, but it ended in disappointment as Steven Gerrard headed into his own net ten minutes from time and Chelsea proved too strong in extra time as goals from Drogba and Kezman rendered Antonio Nunez's headed goal irrelevant. It was Chelsea who landed the first major honour of the season – but our time was to come.

Scott Carson made his Liverpool debut at Newcastle but could do little to prevent Laurent Robert's curling free kick giving the Magpies all three points.

MARCH

If the Premiership was continuing to be a frustrating experience for Rafael Benitez then the Champions League was giving him much more pleasure as he watched his side triumph 3-1 in Leverkusen to secure a 6-2 aggregate win and book a place in the last eight of the tournament.

After a goalless draw with Blackburn all the talk was of the biggest Merseyside derby in years as the two local rivals battled for fourth place and the final automatic qualifying spot for the Champions League. It was a game Liverpool needed to win, and that they did thanks to a blistering start which brought goals from Steven Gerrard and Luis Garcia. Tim Cahill pulled one back for the Blues late on but they couldn't force an equaliser and it was the red half of the city left to claim local bragging rights.

Igor Biscan's late header secured another vital Premiership victory over Bolton Wanderers before Liverpool turned to the job of trying to upset the odds and knock Italian giants Juventus out of the Champions League.

APRIL

Juventus had conceded just two goals in the competition prior to arriving on Merseyside but Liverpool doubled that tally within 25 minutes as goals from Sami Hyypia and Luis Garcia sent the home fans into dreamland. Only a late consolation strike from Cannavaro could take the shine off another glorious European night.

The league campaign continued to be a source of frustration for the fans as defeat at Manchester City was followed by a draw with Tottenham. Three points were then collected against Portsmouth before Crystal Palace gave their relegation battle a major boost by winning 1-0 at Selhurst Park.

But, brilliantly, in amongst the league problems Liverpool turned in one of their finest European performances for years to prevent Juventus scoring in the Stadio Delle Alpi and progressed to the Champions League semi-finals thanks to a 2-1 aggregate victory.

With the games coming thick and fast it was Chelsea who lay in wait in the semi-final as British football geared up for its biggest battle in years. Chelsea may have been romping towards the Premiership title, but they found Liverpool a tough nut to crack and the Reds left Stamford Bridge at the end of a tight first leg with an impressive goalless draw.

LIVERPOOL ARE THE MOST SUCCESSFUL CLUB IN ENGLIS

The month no Liverpool fan will ever, ever forget.

MAY

The league campaign ended as it had begun, with an inconsistent mix of results forcing manager Rafael Benitez to admit he needed to strengthen his squad in a bid to get closer to the top three next season.

Defeat at Arsenal ultimately cost Liverpool the chance of finishing fourth, although victory over Aston Villa at the end of the season at least ensured the players ended their league campaign on a positive note. Djibril Cisse with the two goals which confirmed his recovery from the broken leg he sustained back in October.

But it was the Champions League campaign which was dominating the thoughts of all Liverpool fans as Chelsea arrived at Anfield for the second leg of their semi final clash.

Chelsea had beaten the Reds three times already during the season but when Luis Garcia opened the scoring after just six minutes at Anfield there was a real belief that Liverpool were going to make it all the way to Istanbul. And after Eidur Gudjohnsen missed a sitter in the final minute Anfield went crazy as the referee sounded his final whistle to signal the Reds' first appearance in a European Cup final for 20 years.

The final with AC Milan will go down in history as one of the greatest matches in the competition.

Dead and seemingly buried at half time as the classy Italians strolled into a three goal lead, Liverpool emerged for the second period desperate to restore some pride.

When Steven Gerrard headed home after 51 minutes there was a glimmer of hope. When Vladimir Smicer smashed home a low shot two minutes later there was a belief. When Xabi Alonso converted a penalty on the rebound shortly after there were scenes like you've never seen before as thousands of jubilant Reds' fans celebrated wildly and struggled to take in what the previous six minutes had served up.

The rest, as they say, is history as Liverpool held on throughout extra time, thanks largely to a heroic defensive performance and the brilliance of Jerzy Dudek in the Liverpool goal. He somehow kept out Andriy Shevchenko's late close range strike, to set up a penalty shoot out.

Liverpool had established a 3-2 lead in the shoot-out competition when Shevchenko was again foiled by Dudek to trigger scenes of ecstacy both on the pitch and in the stands. Liverpool were crowned European Champions for the fifth time in their illustrious history.

It certainly was a season to remember!

The Champions League QUIZ 2004-05

1. Who did Liverpool beat in the qualifying round of the competition?

2. Which three teams made up Liverpool's group?

3. Who scored our first goal in the group stages of the competition?

4. How many group games did we lose?

5. Who scored our second goal against Olympiacos at Anfield?

6. Who was our top Champions League goalscorer?

7. What was the aggregate score against Bayer Leverkusen in the last 16 of the Champions League?

8. Who scored our first goal against Juventus?

9. Who missed a sitter for Chelsea in the final minute of the semi-final at Anfield?

10. What was the final score in the penalty shoot-out v AC Milan?

PART ONE

JUST HOW MUCH DO YOU REALLY KNOW ABOUT LIVERPOOL FOOTBALL CLUB?

1. Where did Liverpool sign Josemi from?

2. Where did Liverpool sign Luis Garcia from?

3. Against which team did Michael Owen score his final goal for Liverpool?

4. Who knocked Liverpool out of the Carling Cup last season?

5. With which team did Stephen Warnock win a fans player of the year award?

6. Against who did Xabi Alonso score his first goal for Liverpool?

7. Against who did Djibril Cisse score his first goal at Anfield?

8. Against who did Luis Garcia score his first goal for LFC?

9. Who left Liverpool for Charlton Athletic in 2004?

10. Who is Liverpool's Assistant manager?

11. Against which team did David Raven make his LFC debut?

12. Against who did Stephen Warnock make his first start for Liverpool?

1. Jerzy's penalty save from Andriy Shevchenko in the Champions League final won the European Cup for Liverpool.

2. Jerzy names Peter Schmeichel as his all time goalkeeping hero.

3. His amazing double save from Andriy Shevchenko in the closing stages of the Champions League final has been described as one of the finest stops of all time.

4. Jerzy has admitted he would probably have followed his father's career and become a Polish miner had he not found a career in football.

5. He signed for Liverpool on the final day of August in 2001 – on the same day as Chris Kirkland.

6. He played just 15 games for little known Polish club Sokol Tychy before moving to Dutch side Feyenoord.

7. He quickly became a cult hero in Rotterdam, and during the 1998/99 season was voted the best keeper in the Dutch League.

8. He kept 26 clean sheets during a highly impressive first season at Liverpool.

9. He was named man of the match for the Reds in their Worthington Cup victory over Manchester United in 2003.

10. He is first choice goalkeeper for his country and represented Poland during the 2002 World Cup finals.

JERZY DUDEK

1

1. Steven Gerrard v Olympiacos December 8 2004 - Champions League

How the goal was scored: With Liverpool four minutes away from going out of the competition, Neil Mellor glanced the ball into Gerrard's path and the skipper sent Anfield into delirium with a 20 yard right footed volley into the far corner of the Kop net.

What Gerrard said: "It was probably the best goal I have ever scored. As soon as I made contact with the ball I knew I was going to at least work the goalkeeper. It was such a sweet strike and to see the ball fly into the corner was a brilliant feeling".

2. Luis Garcia v Juventus
April 5 2004 - Champions League

How the goal was scored: Anthony Le Tallec lofted the ball into Garcia's path and the Spaniard beat Juventus goalkeeper Buffon with a brilliant dipping volley from 25 yards to give the Reds a two goal lead.

What Garcia said: "It was an amazing feeling to see the ball go into the net. It was such an important game for us and so to gain an early 2-0 lead was brilliant. That was probably my best ever goal. I really enjoyed it".

3. Steven Gerrard v Middlesbrough April 30 2004 - Barclays Premiership

How the goal was scored: Another corker from the captain as he blasted a swerving, dipping volley over the out-stretched arms of the Middlesbrough goalkeeper and into the back of the net from the right angle of the penalty area.

What Gerrard said: "I enjoyed the goal but at the end of the day we haven't won the game and so I'm a bit disappointed. It was a decent strike and I was pleased to score another goal, but I'd have enjoyed it even more if it had brought three points".

4. Xabi Alonso v Arsenal November 28 2004 - Barclays Premiership

How the goal was scored: Gerrard slipped the ball into Alonso's path on the edge of the area and the Liverpool midfielder made no mistake with a crashing shot which flew beyond Jens Lehmann and into the roof of the Anfield Road net.

What Alonso said: "It was a good team move and I managed to make a run to the edge of the box without an Arsenal player tracking me. When the ball arrived at my feet all I wanted to do was keep the shot on target. I couldn't have hit it any better".

5. Neil Mellor v Arsenal 28 November 2004 - Barclays Premiership

How the goal was scored: Harry Kewell glanced Chris Kirkland's long kick into the path of Mellor who made no mistake with a low shot from 20 yards which flew into the far corner of the net and gave Liverpool victory with the last kick of the match.

What Mellor said: "That was the highlight of my career so far. To score a goal like that in a game like that against the champions in the final minute was just a dream come true. I can't wait to watch it again and again on television".

RAFAEL BENITEZ IS LIVERPOOL'S ELEVENTH POST-WAR MANAGER.

RAFAEL BENITEZ

Despite only having been in the managerial hot-seat for little over a year, Rafael Benitez has already written his name into Anfield folklore.

Last season's stunning Champions League triumph has elevated the name of Benitez alongside the likes of Shankly, Paisley, Fagan and Dalglish as Liverpool managers who have brought the good times to Anfield.

Last year was supposed to be one of transition for the Spaniard as he got to grips with life in a new country and with a new group of players. It certainly wasn't expected to end with Steven Gerrard proudly lifting the most glittering prize in European club football.

So what next for Rafa? How can he possibly better what he candidly describes as "the biggest achievement of my footballing life?"

"It was great to win the trophy," he says. "There were times during the competition when maybe we thought we were going out, but the players kept fighting until the end and got their reward."

"I always go into competitions to win. That's always my idea. I don't play to come second, third or fourth. I play to win."

"I'm so proud of what the players did in the Champions League last season and their names will now go down in the club's history. They should be proud of themselves for that."

"We had to beat some good teams along the way and nobody can ever say we had it easy. But we fought and battled until the very end and finished up as champions. It was a magnificent achievement and I'll remember that night in Istanbul for the rest of my life."

The sensational victory over AC Milan in the Ataturk Stadium not only saw Liverpool clinch the trophy for the fifth time, it also re-established the Reds as a major force in the European game.

And as Benitez gradually begins to shape the squad he wants for a prolonged period of success on Merseyside, he admits the triumph couldn't have come at a better time.

He said: "The interesting thing now is that players want to come and play for us. They see we are a good team with good players. We have a winning mentality and that makes it easier for me as a manager to persuade players to come to the club."

"We are still at the start of our project. My idea is to be here for a long time and win more trophies for the fans."

"Of course some of the players who played in the final aren't with us anymore but they have left with their heads held high. I told the group before the game that if some of them were playing their last game for us then they should try and leave as a European champion."

"I am the manager and it is my responsibility to make the decisions. Sometimes tough decisions need to be made but if you don't address them then you don't move forward."

"We have a very clear idea about the future and about the way we want to take this club. I know the kind of standard I want in the team and we will work as hard as possible to get there."

Despite ending the season on an unbelievable high, Benitez is well aware that Liverpool's Premiership record left a lot to be desired last year.

Thirteen defeats – ten away from Anfield – was a disappointing record which ultimately cost the Reds fourth place in the table as they were pipped in the race for Champions League qualification by Mersey neighbours Everton, and the manager intends improving on that statistic this time around.

He said: "It's not normal to lose so many games away from home. There were so many times last season when we came away from a game and I said to myself 'how did we lose that match?' We were losing to teams who weren't better than us and it was very frustrating."

"If you aren't playing well and can't win the game then you have to make sure you don't lose it. There were too many games which we lost by a single goal."

"We need to show the right mentality away from home. We need players who will fight and battle in every game. Our home form is usually good, in fact we played a number of high quality games at Anfield last season, but away from home we struggled and didn't pick up anywhere near as many points as we should have done."

"Okay, we won the Champions League and it was brilliant for the club but I was still very disappointed with what we did in the league. Our inconsistency throughout the season was very frustrating but I can tell you it'll be different this year."

"I've been here for a year now and I know the league, the players and the referees much better. It's been a learning experience for me and I'll be better for it."

"We were more than 30 points behind the champions at the end of the season and we want to close that gap this year. We will close that gap, I am sure about that. We won't lose as many games this year. It won't happen."

Benitez may not promise a title success next season to follow on from last year's European glory, but he insists he'll do all he can to help bring more smiles to the faces of Kopites all over the world.

He added: "For me, Liverpool supporters are the best in the world. They are incredible. The scenes when we brought the European Cup back from Turkey will stay with me forever."

"My wife reads a lot about the history of the club and she is always telling me how important it is to be successful for the fans."

"Our supporters are always with us and that is something I didn't experience in Valencia. The fans would shout my name towards the end, but at the start it took a while to win them over. Here, from the very first day they supported me and I thank them for that."

"As I said earlier, my staff and I have a clear vision for this club. We know what we want to do and we know how to get there. It may take time but we will work as hard as we can to win more trophies."

"Last season we reached two finals, won one of them and lost the other. This season we will be entering four competitions and it will be my idea to win them all. This club is all about winning trophies. Last year was a great start, especially because it meant the club can now keep the European Cup forever, but we have to look forward and enjoy the challenge of winning Cups on a regular basis."

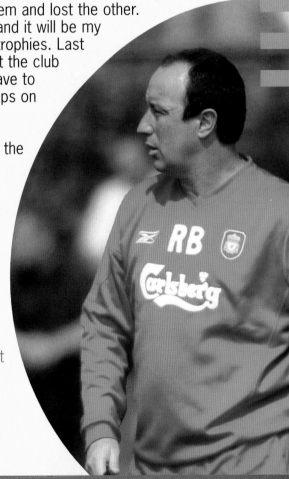

"I want to be here for a long time to do that. I hear the rumours about other jobs but I can assure all the fans that I want to stay at Liverpool. I have a long contract, I am happy here, the board has faith in me, the supporters are backing me so why would I want to go anywhere?"

"My idea is to be here for many, many years and try to achieve the kind of success past managers have at the club."

"I may have won the European Cup but I'm not at the level yet of the likes of Shankly and Paisley. But I'll work as hard as I can to get there."

JUST HOW MUCH DO YOU REALLY KNOW ABOUT LIVERPOOL FOOTBALL CLUB?

13 Which LFC legend has a book out called Ghost of Anfield?

14 Which former LFC striker is a famous football commentator/presenter in Spain?

15 Who did Steve Finnan score his first goal for LFC against?

16 How many goals did Milan Baros score in Euro 2004?

17 Which LFC legend scored two winning goals in a European Cup Final?

18 Which team did Rafael Benitez leave to join Liverpool after guiding them to a La Liga title?

19 With which club did Rafael Benitez begin his coaching career?

20 In which city was Rafael Benitez born?

21 Which LFC hero was nicknamed Crazy Horse?

22 From which club did Liverpool sign Mauricio Pellegrino?

23 What squad number did Kevin Keegan and Kenny Dalglish make famous at Anfield?

24 Who scored Liverpool's penalties in the Champions League shoot-out with AC Milan?

1. Despite speculation he was about to leave Liverpool at the start of last season, Steve has established himself as first choice right back under Rafael Benitez.

2. Steve was signed by Gerard Houllier from Fulham in the summer of 2003.

3. Steve was recommended to Liverpool by former striker Karl-Heinz Riedle who enjoyed a spell on the coaching staff at Craven Cottage.

4. The Republic of Ireland defender represented his country during their 2002 World Cup campaign in Japan and South Korea.

5. Steve started his career at non-league Welling before moving into league football with Birmingham under Barry Fry.

6. He was signed for Fulham by ex-Anfield leg end Kevin Keegan.

7. Steve netted one goal for the Reds last season – an individual effort against West Bromwich at Anfield.

8. He was born in the Irish county of Limerick.

9. He has so far managed just the one goal for his country.

10. Only Jamie Carragher and John Arne Riise made more appearances than Steve during last season.

STEVE FINNAN

3

IAN RUSH IS THE CLUB'S RECORD SCORER WITH 346 GOALS.

Premiership

Played: 38
Won: 17
Drew: 7
Lost: 14
Goal Difference: +12
Position: 5th

F.A. Cup

Went out 1-0 at 3rd round stage to first division Burnley at Turf Moor.

Carling Cup

Defeated Millwall, Middlesbrough, Tottenham and Watford before losing 3-2 to Chelsea after extra time in the final at Cardiff's Millennium Stadium.

Champions League

An epic run to the final which resulted in one of the most glorious nights in the club's history as the Reds overcame AC Milan in a penalty shoot-out to win the trophy for the fifth time.

MICHAEL OWEN HOLDS THE RECORD FOR MOST GOALS IN EUROPE FO

Top Scorers

Milan Baros: 13
Luis Garcia: 13
Steven Gerrard: 13
John Arne Riise: 8
Djibril Cisse: 5
Neil Mellor: 5
Florent Sinama-Pongolle: 4

Most Appearances

John Arne Riise: 57
Jamie Carragher: 56
Steve Finnan: 51
Sami Hyypia: 49
Milan Baros: 45

HE REDS AFTER FINDING THE NET 22 TIMES.

1. Sami began his career with the little known MyPa Anjalankoski, with whom he helped win the Finnish Cup in 1992.

2. He made his international debut against Tunisia and his consistent form attracted the attentions of Dutch outfit Willem II, who secured his services in 1995.

3. He was signed by Gerard Houllier in 1999 and went on to establish an excellent defensive partnership with Stephane Henchoz.

4. In the absence of injured skipper Jamie Redknapp and vice-captain Robbie Fowler, Sami assumed the role of captain, and led the Reds out in both the FA and UEFA Cup Final's in 2001. He also captained the side in the Charity Shield victory over Manchester United and the Super Cup success against Bayern Munich.

5. In 2001 he went through the entire campaign without collecting a single red or yellow card – an amazing statistic for a defender.

6. He was handed the captaincy at Anfield on a full time basis in April 2002.

7. Sami has played more than 300 games for the Reds and has chipped in with more than 20 goals. Not a bad return at all!

8. Only Jamie Carragher, John Arne Riise and Steve Finnan played more games for Liverpool than Sami last season.

9. He lost his place in the team for a short while last year to Mauricio Pellegrino, but soon won it back and was immense during the Champions League campaign.

10. Sami became the first Finn to play a professional game for the Reds when he signed in from Willem II.

SAMI HYYPIA

4

30

1. Reds signed the French defender from Laval in February 1999.

2. He made his debut for Liverpool in a League Cup tie at Hull City.

3. He spent a season on loan at Lens during the 2001/2002 campaign when he teamed up again with former Liverpool coach Patrice Bergues.

4. He has played most of his games for the Reds under Rafael Benitez as a left back, despite starting his career in the centre of defence.

5. He says he likes to spend time away from football listening to a wide range of music including hip-hop and garage.

6. He has been capped at full international level by Mali.

7. His Premier debut for the Reds came in a 1-0 victory over Bradford at Anfield.

8. He scored his first goal for the Reds in a European tie in Bucharest during the 2003-04 season.

9. Rafael Benitez described Djimi as one of the club's most improved performers during last season.

10. AC Milan, Paris St Germain and Lazio were just three of the clubs chasing Djimi before he opted to sign for Liverpool.

DJIMI TRAORE

21

LIVERPOOL BY NUMBERS

1. How many European Cups have Liverpool won?

2. In which year did we last win the championship?

3. What is our record attendance at Anfield?

4. What squad number did Jamie Carragher wear in the Champions League final in Istanbul?

5. How many league games did Liverpool win last season?

6. How many goals did we score in the Premiership last season?

7. And how many did we concede?

8. How many points did Everton finish above us in the final table?

9. In which year was Liverpool FC formed?

10. In which year did the roof go on the famous Spion Kop?

PHIL NEAL WON 20 MEDALS DURING HIS ANFIELD CAREER – MORE THAN AN

1. John Arne played his 200th game for Liverpool last season, only four years after moving to Anfield.

2. He captained his country for the first time in June when he led Norway out for a friendly match with Sweden. To add the icing on the cake on his night to remember, he scored the opening goal for Norway.

3. He has a reputation as a free scoring midfield player after netting eight goals during his first season with Liverpool.

4. After spending most of his Liverpool career under Gerard Houllier as a left back, he is now usually employed on the left side of midfield.

5. He only missed one Premiership game last season.

6. Before signing for Liverpool he was named as Norway's 'Athlete of the Year' for 2001.

7. He has admitted he almost signed for Fulham before Liverpool came in to secure his services.

8. The famous 'How did you score that goal?' song in his honour was born after a wonder strike against Manchester United during his debut season at Liverpool.

9. John Arne won the league championship in France with Monaco before coming to Merseyside.

10. John Arne was rewarded with a new contract extension in the summer of 2002 which ties him to Anfield until 2007.

6 JOHN ARNE RIISE

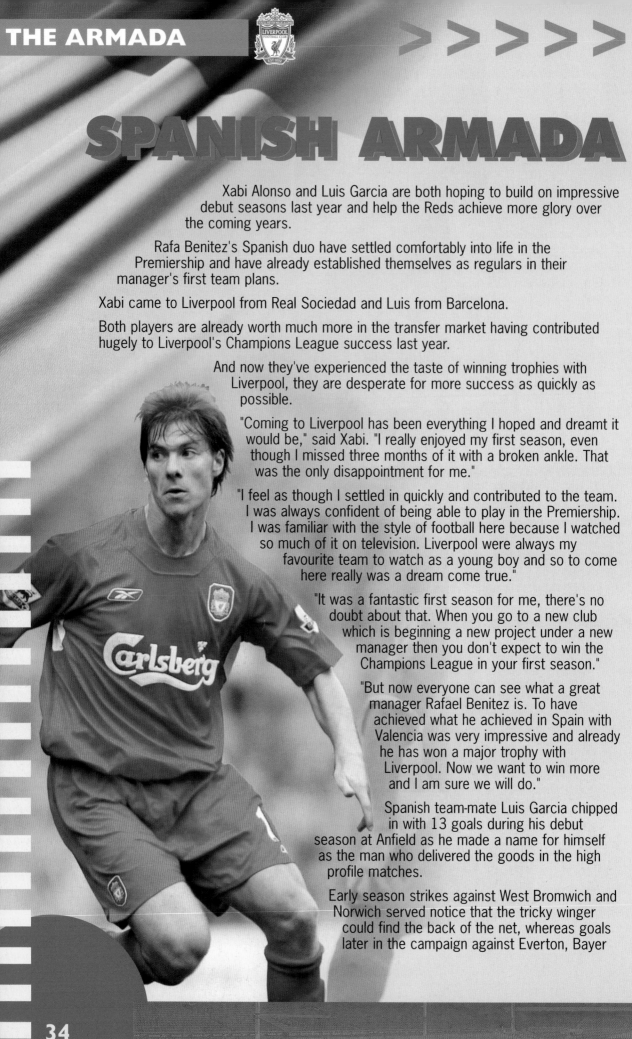

SPANISH ARMADA

Xabi Alonso and Luis Garcia are both hoping to build on impressive debut seasons last year and help the Reds achieve more glory over the coming years.

Rafa Benitez's Spanish duo have settled comfortably into life in the Premiership and have already established themselves as regulars in their manager's first team plans.

Xabi came to Liverpool from Real Sociedad and Luis from Barcelona.

Both players are already worth much more in the transfer market having contributed hugely to Liverpool's Champions League success last year.

And now they've experienced the taste of winning trophies with Liverpool, they are desperate for more success as quickly as possible.

"Coming to Liverpool has been everything I hoped and dreamt it would be," said Xabi. "I really enjoyed my first season, even though I missed three months of it with a broken ankle. That was the only disappointment for me."

"I feel as though I settled in quickly and contributed to the team. I was always confident of being able to play in the Premiership. I was familiar with the style of football here because I watched so much of it on television. Liverpool were always my favourite team to watch as a young boy and so to come here really was a dream come true."

"It was a fantastic first season for me, there's no doubt about that. When you go to a new club which is beginning a new project under a new manager then you don't expect to win the Champions League in your first season."

"But now everyone can see what a great manager Rafael Benitez is. To have achieved what he achieved in Spain with Valencia was very impressive and already he has won a major trophy with Liverpool. Now we want to win more and I am sure we will do."

Spanish team-mate Luis Garcia chipped in with 13 goals during his debut season at Anfield as he made a name for himself as the man who delivered the goods in the high profile matches.

Early season strikes against West Bromwich and Norwich served notice that the tricky winger could find the back of the net, whereas goals later in the campaign against Everton, Bayer

Leverkusen, Juventus and Chelsea elevated him to 'Kop hero' status.

"I've always scored goals during my career and so I'm not surprised I was able to do well," he said. "But I know I should have scored even more because I did miss some chances in some games. Next year I want to score more goals if possible because I know what I am capable of."

"It was hard for me at the start of the season because I found the physical side of English football a bit difficult to come to terms with. I expected that to be the case because I had been told that the Premiership is a fast, tough league. But I was taken aback slightly by just how demanding it is from a physical point of view."

"Now I'm one year older and one year wiser. I know what it's all about and I'll be better prepared for it in the future."

"I've done a lot of work building up my strength and so I am sure the Liverpool fans will see an even better Luis Garcia this season. That's my aim."

"This club is so special and the fans are brilliant. I get goosebumps when they sing You'll Never Walk Alone. It's an amazing experience and I'm so proud to be a part of it."

"Under Rafa Liverpool is going in the right direction, there's no question about that. He knows how to create a winning team, as the Champions League showed last year, and he'll now be working harder than ever to make sure we move on from that success and win more trophies in the future. It's an exciting time for the club and a great time to be a Liverpool player."

As far as Rafa himself is concerned, he's more than pleased with the contributions of his Spanish duo so far.

He said: "We missed Xabi when he was out for three months because he is the sort of player who can control a game. He is a clever, intelligent player. You always need your best players to be on the field and we did miss him.

"Luis has always scored goals – he even did when he played for me at Tenerife – and so what he achieved last season didn't surprise me. But the challenge for him now, and for the rest of the team, is to build on what we have achieved and look to be more consistent in our play, especially away from home in the league."

For season 2005-2006, Junior members of the Official Liverpool Supporters Club will receive a fantastic range of benefits and offers. There's an exclusive Liverpool FC teddy bear, a Junior Member's magazine, which is full of player pictures and brilliant prizes! Also included is a Liverpool FC pencil case and school kit including a ruler, pencil, pencil sharpener and rubber to make sure all your class mates know you are a supporter of the best team in the world.

You could be one of the lucky ones chosen to lead out the Reds at an away Premiership match and be Liverpool FC's mascot for the game. There's also the chance to come along to the Junior Members Xmas party, held here at Anfield!

If you would like to become a Junior member of the best Club in the world, ring 08707 020207 or visit www.liverpoolfc.tv

Junior Membership:

- Free Fan Card if required.
- Quarterly Member Magazines inc. exclusive competitions and player features.
- Liverpool FC teddy bear.
- Liverpool pencil case and school kit.
- Chance to be a mascot at an away match.
- Chance to attend the Xmas Party at Anfield.
- 10% off merchandise in official club stores.
- Monthly Mega Draw.
- 2 for 1 museum offer.
- Exclusive LFC Magazine Offers.

PRICE: £19.95 inc P&P
£2 discount if paying by direct debit.

IDENTIFY YOUR FAVOURITE LIVERPOOL PLAYERS
Look carefully at the ten photos below and see if you
can identify the players from these picture clues.

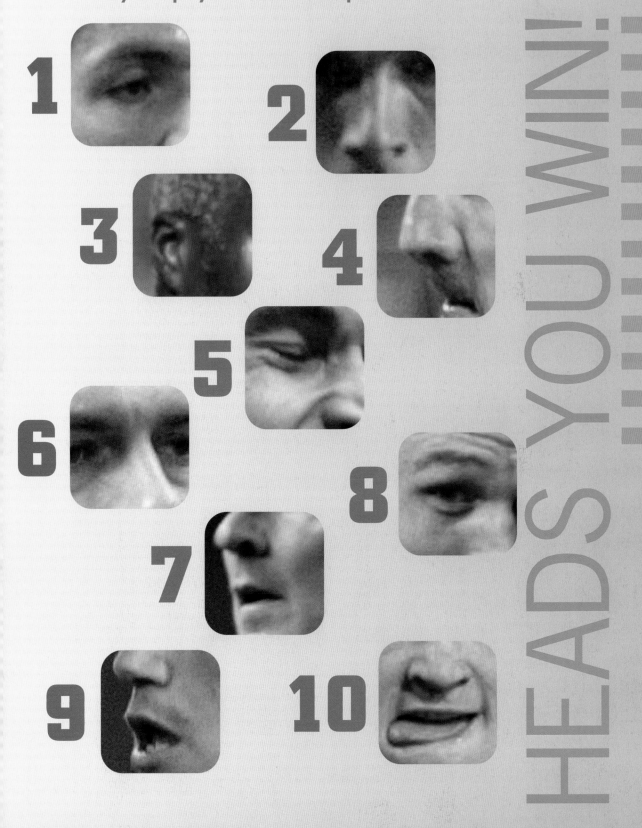

HEADS YOU WIN!

1. Steven became the fourth Liverpool captain to lift the European Cup following the Reds' victory over AC Milan in Istanbul.

2. He captained his country for the first time against Sweden before Euro 2004.

3. He made his Liverpool debut in November 1998 against Blackburn as a substitute.

4. His full debut for the Reds came against Celta Vigo at Anfield in the UEFA Cup.

5. Gerard Houllier handed him the Anfield captaincy in October 2003 ahead of a European clash with Olimpija Ljubljana.

6. Steven came up through the youth ranks at Anfield and is a product of the LFC Academy.

7. He was a Liverpool fan as a boy and names his favourite players as John Barnes and Ronnie Whelan.

8. He is now an established member of the England team.

9. The Premiership title is the only major club honour to have eluded Steven in his Liverpool career so far.

10. He averaged a goal every four games last season as he once again reached double figures in terms of goals scored.

STEVEN GERRARD

8

1. Didi turned down offers from Bolton and Hamburg to sign a new Liverpool contract last summer.

2. His sparkling end of season form, including his brilliant display in the Champions League final, helped persuade the manager to keep him at Anfield.

3. Didi is in the record books for being the player who scored the final ever goal at the old Wembley when he netted for Germany against England in October 2000.

4. He started his career with little

   known German club Wacker Munich, where his father was the coach.

5. He joined Bayern Munich as a 16 year old in 1989 and made his debut two years later.

6. In nine years with Bayern he won two Bundesliga titles, the German Cup and the UEFA Cup.

7. Kenny Dalglish took him to Newcastle from Munich in 1998. He signed for Liverpool a year later after the Reds won a race with Barcelona and Arsenal for his services.

8. Didi became the first Liverpool player since Roger Hunt in 1966 to play in a World Cup final when he lined up for Germany against Brazil in 2002.

9. He cites horse racing as being his favourite pastime away from the game.

10. Didi has played more than 250 games for the Reds but has only just managed to reach double figures in terms of goals scored.

DIETMAR HAMANN

16

LIVERPOOL'S MIRACLE MAN DJIBRIL CISSE

Liverpool's own miracle man has promised Kopites everywhere that we'll see him back at his goalscoring best this season.

Djibril Cisse isn't just back fully fit again after returning towards the end of last season, he's back with a promise that he'll make up for lost time and bang in the goals for Rafa Benitez during the course of this campaign.

The fact that Djibril is even playing football again owes much to the expertise of Liverpool's medical staff who guided him back to fitness after breaking his leg in two places at Blackburn in October 2004.

There were those who said he'd never play again after the injury he sustained at Ewood Park, but the player himself was never in any doubt he'd make a full recovery.

"While I was in hospital I heard people say on the television and in the newspapers that I was finished and I found that funny," he said. "These people don't know me. I know me and I knew I'd be back."

"I was surprised to play at the end of last season because I thought I'd be out for a lot longer, but the medical staff at Liverpool have been brilliant with me and I owe them a lot."

"It was something of a miracle that I was back so soon. I worked very hard during my rehabilitation programme and focused completely on getting back as soon as I could. I set myself small goals along the way and then after just six months I was back again."

"It was a pity last season ended when it did because I was just starting to get my sharpness back. It always takes a while after you've been out for so long and I could have done with the season going on for an extra few weeks."

Djibril's campaign ended gloriously in Istanbul as he helped the Reds secure the Champions League trophy with victory over AC Milan. Having netted a double against Aston Villa on the last weekend of the Premiership season he then had the confidence to step up and take one of the crucial spot kicks in the European shoot-out.

He said: "The goals against Villa gave me a boost and I was confident about taking the penalty in Istanbul. Of course I was nervous as well because I knew how much was riding on it and how much it meant to the club."

"To win the Champions League last season was a great achievement and really goes to show the potential we have here."

"Rafa Benitez has shown himself to be a great manager already and for me he is the best in the country. To win the Champions League in his first year at Liverpool was amazing. Truly amazing."

"Now we have to go on from here and win more trophies for this great club and for the supporters."

"We know we let ourselves and the fans down in the Premiership last year and we have to improve. The manager knows that and the players know it. I'm sure we'll be better this year."

"As far as I'm concerned I'm just glad to be back playing again. I missed a lot of last season and I'm keen to make up for lost time now."

"While I was out everyone at this club showed they care for me. The players were always asking how I was and it was the same whenever I met fans on the streets. I know how much people care for me and that means everything."

"The best way I can pay them back is by scoring lots of goals this season and that's what I aim to do."

"My injury came just as I was settling into English football. I was feeling good and starting to score goals but then injury struck at Blackburn. I always knew it wouldn't be the end of me and this season I want to pay back every person who has shown such faith in me."

DJIBRIL CISSE

9

1. Xabi was born in Spain on 25th November 1981.

2. He built a reputation as one of the most promising central midfielders in La Liga. He has vision, is comfortable on the ball and can score goals.

3. Xabi came through the youth ranks at Real Sociedad and made his debut for the San Sebastian outfit in the 1999/2000 season.

4. The following season in 2000/2001 Xabi spent the first part of the campaign on loan at minnows SD Eibar before returning to Real Sociedad later that season to break into the team.

5. Season 2002/2003 was the campaign when Xabi came to prominence as a star in the making and was a key performer as Real finished second in La Liga behind champions Real Madrid.

6. Xabi was called up to the Spain national team for the first time in 2003 and made his debut at the age of 21 in a 4-0 friendly win over Ecuador.

7. One of Xabi's all time heroes is ex-Red John Aldridge following their joint association with Spanish outfit Real Sociedad.

8. He made his full debut for Spain in a Euro 2004 2-1 qualifying win over Ukraine.

9. Last season Xabi played 35 games for Real Sociedad and although it wasn't a great season domestically scored a memorable goal against Valencia, giving Rafael Benitez a close glimpse of his undoubted talent.

10. Xabi comes from a famous footballing family. His dad Miguel Angel 'Periko' Alonso was a star for Barcelona and won two league titles with Real Sociedad. Xabi's brother, fellow midfielder Mikel Alonso, is also on Real Sociedad's books.

XABI ALONSO

14

EPHRAIM LONGWORTH WENT AN INCREDIBLE 371 GAMES WITHOUT SCORIN

Taking Europe by storm

It started off in the unglamorous surroundings of AK Graz's Arnold Schwarzenegger Stadium and ended up in the Ataturk Stadium in Turkey with Steven Gerrard lifting the biggest prize in club football proudly above his head.

It took Liverpool fifteen games against eight different teams to secure their fifth European Cup – and this is how they did it...

SINGLE GOAL FOR THE REDS.

GAK 0 - 2 LIVERPOOL
10 August 2004 - Champions League Qualifier

While the eyes of the world's media were trained on Michael Owen sitting on the Liverpool bench, the players Rafael Benitez did pick to start the game ensured the former Valencia boss got off to the best possible start in the Kop hot seat with a 2-nil win.

Benitez's team could have been four goals up before Steven Gerrard secured a vital away goal midway through the first-half at the Arnold Schwarzenegger Stadium. When the ball fell to the skipper outside the area, Steven rifled an unstoppable strike towards goal that gave the goalkeeper absolutely no chance.

LIVERPOOL 0 - 1 GAK
24 August 2004 - Champions League Qualifier (2)

The goal by the Austrian side certainly rocked the atmosphere at Anfield. The goal came from a half-cleared corner only to find the foot of Mario Tokic who fired an unstoppable shot into the top corner of the Anfield Road net.

Despite the obvious disappointment of losing this second leg, Liverpool were through to the group stages of the Champions League.

LIVERPOOL 2 - 0 MONACO
15 September 2004 - Champions League Group Phase

The disappointment of losing to Graz was short lived as Liverpool brushed aside Monaco with ease. Djibril Cisse's first Anfield goal - after just 22 minutes - sent the Reds on their way to a memorable European victory. Steven Gerrard played a sublime pass through to the striker's feet and with just Flavio Roma to beat in the Monaco goal, Cisse fired a low shot at goal leaving Roma with no chance.

Benitez's Red army sealed the three points when Baros finished with a sweetly struck left-footed shot into the corner of the net.

OLYMPIACOS 1 - 0 LIVERPOOL
28 September 2004 - Champions League Group Phase

Liverpool's travel troubles continued in Athens when they lost for the first time on Greek soil. The half-time statistics told the whole story when they reported the fact that the home side had 13 efforts on goal compared to just two - both of which were off-target - for the visitors.

The first and only goal of the match came after just 7 minutes when Leroklis Stoltidis rose high to meet

Rivaldo's in swinging free-kick and head the ball beyond the helpless Jerzy Dudek.

LIVERPOOL 0 - 0 DEPORTIVO LA CORUNA
19 October 2004 - Champions League Group Phase

Liverpool were made to rue a host of missed first half chances as they were held to a 0-0 draw by a brave Deportivo La Coruna. Both Djibril Cisse and Milan Baros were left scratching their heads after unleashing shot after shot only to be denied by the Deportivo 'keeper Jose Molina.

The Reds still looked favourites to go on and take the lead as they increased the pressure but in the end it was a frustrating night for Liverpool.

DEPORTIVO LA CORUNA 0 - 1 LIVERPOOL
03 November 2004 - Champions League Group Phase

A massive boost for Liverpool as a first-half own goal by Jorge Andrade was enough to give the Reds a deserved three points at the Riazor and ensure their first win in Spain for 21 years.

Liverpool might have doubled their lead after 82 minutes through Luis Garcia but in the end it didn't matter as Liverpool travelled home with three precious points in their pocket.

MONACO 1 - 0 LIVERPOOL
23 November 2004 - Champions League Group Phase

Liverpool's Champions League qualification hopes took a turn for the worse inside the Louis II stadium in Monaco as Rafael Benitez's side were beaten by a solitary second-half goal from Javier Pedro Saviola.

The 2,500 travelling Liverpool supporters had to suffer the sight of two of their heroes being stretchered off down the tunnel in front of them. With the Reds already missing Djibril Cisse and Milan Baros, the injury crisis deepened as Luis Garcia and Josemi were both carried off.

Saviola opened the scoring while appearing to handle the ball inside the area before sending his shot past Kirkland.

LIVERPOOL 3 - 1 OLYMPIACOS
08 December 2004 - Champions League Group Phase

One of the finest moments of Liverpool's history in European football as Anfield witnessed second-half goals from Florent Sinama-Pongolle, Neil Mellor and Steven Gerrard to cancel out a first half free-kick by Rivaldo to complete an incredible comeback and raise the roof off a euphoric Kop.

When Rivaldo gave Olympiacos the lead against the run of play, it seemed almost impossible for the Reds to qualify to the knock-out stages. With a win by two clear goals required, Liverpool certainly had to do something special after the interval. Whatever Rafa said at half-time, it worked.

An early strike by Pongolle was followed by another from Mellor but the best was saved for a thrilling climax with an absolute screamer from Gerrard with only minutes to go sealing the 2-goal advantage. Liverpool were heading for the last 16.

LIVERPOOL 3 - 1 BAYER 04 LEVERKUSEN
22 February 2005 - Champions League last 16

Liverpool had one foot in the quarter-final of the Champions League after goals from Luis Garcia, John Arne Riise and Didi Hamann secured a 3-1 first leg advantage against Bayer Leverkusen at Anfield.

With Steven Gerrard suspended and Fernando Morientes ineligible, no one expected Liverpool to race into a two-goal lead so early but it was not all one-way traffic. The threat of an away goal lurked throughout a tense second-half and although Dietmar Hamann converted a 25-yard free kick on the 90th minute, the Reds were hit by a late Franca strike to keep the tie alive.

BAYER 04 LEVERKUSEN 1 - 3 LIVERPOOL
09 March 2005 - Champions League last 16

Liverpool stamped their mark on the competition by beating Leverkusen once again by 3 goals to 1 (6-2 on aggregate).

Once Garcia opened the scoring in the 26th minute, it looked like game over but it wasn't long before the Spaniard hit home again from a second corner taken by Gerrard. Baros executed an emphatic volley late on and even a late consolation strike for Jacek Krzynowek couldn't take the shine off job well done by Rafa's side.

LIVERPOOL 2 - 1 JUVENTUS
05 April 2005 - Champions League Quarter-Final

A slender lead to take to Turin but a win all the same. Early goals from Sami Hyypia and Luis Garcia gave the Reds an early upper hand and it seemed that the flying start was going to pay-off until Juventus grabbed the crucial away goal after the interval through defender Fabio Cannavaro.

Liverpool took the lead just after 10-minutes when Garcia flicked the ball over the Juventus defence for Sami Hyypia at the back post to volley past Gianluigi Buffon. And if Hyypia's opener had the Kop on its feet, Luis Garcia's second after 25 minutes lifted the elated fans right off them as he unleashed an unstoppable dipping volley.

JUVENTUS 0 - 0 LIVERPOOL
13 April 2005 - Champions League
Quarter-Final (2)

Liverpool deservedly clinched a place in the last four of the Champions League after heroically holding Juventus to a goal-less draw on a memorable night in Turin.

It was a nail-biting night for both sides but Liverpool held their nerve with Jamie Carragher and Sami Hyypia immense at the back.

When the final whistle came it sparked ecstatic scenes amongst the players and travelling fans. Now a mouth-watering match between Chelsea would decide who goes into the final of the Champions League.

CHELSEA 0 - 0 LIVERPOOL
27 April 2005 - Champions League
Semi-Final (1)

Was it a good result or not? Chelsea were favourites to go through because they stopped Liverpool from scoring an away goal. Rafael Benitez claimed Liverpool were favourites as they'd stopped Chelsea from scoring full stop.

Chelsea created just two openings in the first half but Dudek didn't have a save to make as Liverpool did more than enough to remind Jose Mourinho that they weren't just in London to make up the numbers. Only a late booking for Xabi Alonso, ruling him out of the second leg, could dampen Red spirits on the night.

LIVERPOOL 1 - 0 CHELSEA
03 May 2005 - Champions League Semi-Final (2)

An electric night at Anfield as Liverpool overcame Chelsea in a 1-goal thriller that saw the blues go out to an early Garcia goal.

Only three minutes had passed when Gerrard's flick sent Baros surging clear. He appeared to be brought down by Cech as he prodded the ball past him, but cries for a penalty were quickly replaced by screams of joy as Luis Garcia raced in to put the ball in the Kop net.

The second-half was a nervy affair but Liverpool booked their place in the final. Istanbul here we come!

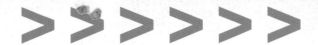

LIVERPOOL 3-3 AC MILAN
(Liverpool win 3-2 on penalties)
25 May 2005 - Champions League Final

Quite simply the best European final of them all and Liverpool's best triumph in this competition.

For the fifth time in the club's glorious history, the gleaming European Cup was heading back to Anfield after the Reds staged the greatest of great comebacks.

Three goals down at the break and being totally outfought and outplayed during a miserable first half in which Hernan Crespo netted twice and Paulo Maldini scored, the Reds emerged a different animal after the half time team talk and quickly went about the job of turning the final on its head.

Within one glorious six minute spell Liverpool had served notice that they were once again a force to be reckoned with on the continent as Steven Gerrard, Vladimir Smicer and Xabi Alonso levelled the game before the hour mark was up.

When Dudek made a fantastic double save to deny Shevchenko in the last minute of extra time you just felt it was going to be Liverpool's night. They were confirmed as European Champions for the fifth time when Shevchenko's penalty was saved by Jerzy Dudek. The Polish keeper had earlier kept out a Pirlo shot and had watched Sergino blast his effort over the bar. Didi Hamann, Vladimir Smicer and Djibril Cisse scored for the Reds in an unforgettable final.

A glorious, glorious night at the end of a never to be forgotten European campaign!

ROGER HUNT HOLDS THE RECORD FOR MOST HAT-TRICKS IN A SEASO

1. Scott was born in Whitehaven on 3rd September 1985 - the night a Ronnie Whelan's brace of goals helped Liverpool to a 2-0 Anfield victory over Nottingham Forest.

2. He was a boyhood Reds fan.

3. Scott was spotted playing for home-town amateur side Cleator Moor Celtic Football Club, and then spent less than a year in the Leeds United Academy and half a season with the reserves before he made his senior debut.

4. He has a string of England youth international honours to his name and is an England Under-21 international with seven caps, the first of which was won against Holland in February 2004.

5. The 19-year-old stands at six foot three and is a good shot stopper. Scott made a dramatic start to his career at Leeds, coming on as a substitute against Middlesbrough in January 2004 after Paul Robinson had been sent off, and then making his full debut two weeks later against Manchester United at Old Trafford last season.

6. Scott made two starts for Leeds in 2003/04 against Manchester United and Chelsea, and played 12 times for the Elland Road reserves.

7. Former Leeds manager Peter Reid describes Scott as a "very good goalkeeper and a terrific prospect."

8. He made his Liverpool debut on March 5 2005 in the 1-0 away defeat at Newcastle. However, he could do little to stop Laurent Robert's winning goal.

9. Scott cites former Leeds number one Paul Robinson as a keeper he'd like to emulate and has ambitions to follow him into the full England squad.

10. He made his Champions League debut for the Reds in the quarter finals last season against Juventus at Anfield.

SCOTT CARSON

20

LIVERPOOL'S PLAYER OF THE YEAR

When captain Steven Gerrard was asked to name Liverpool's Player of the Year at the end of last season he didn't need to think for too long. "Jamie Carragher by a mile," he said. "He's been awesome for us in every game."

Indeed, ask any player who stood out above the rest during the last campaign and the answer will be unanimous.

For years regarded as just another squad member, Jamie Carragher has now established himself as an integral part of Rafa Benitez's plans as well as forcing himself into Sven Goran Eriksson's England squad.

But the Reds' defender admits he thought his Anfield days might have been coming to an end when Benitez arrived at the club in the summer of 2004 and made his first signing.

Carragher says: "The first thing the manager did when he came here was sign Josemi – a right back. At that time I was playing at right back and so of course it crossed my mind that I might struggle to get into the side.

"But in the end the boss moved me to the centre of the defence and things went well for me there. When a new manager arrives and brings in a player who plays in your position then you do wonder, but looking back the season couldn't have gone any better for me."

"I was a regular in the side during the season and felt as though I performed consistently. For a long time I had a reputation as being a versatile player and so it's nice now that I've established myself in one position. It was definitely my best season at the club."

"I know a lot of people have said a lot of nice things about me recently and of course that gives me a confidence boost, but I want to keep working, keep learning and keep improving because that's one thing the manager demands from you."

Carragher admits he's been impressed with Benitez's early days in the Anfield hot seat and has no doubts he's the man to take the club forward.

He said: "He won the Champions League in his first season so what else can you say about him? It's clear already that he's one of the best managers in the game and we're lucky to have him here.

"Jose Mourinho used to like telling people he was the European champion, but he can't say that anymore because Rafael Benitez is."

"What he achieved last season was amazing. I don't think any of us expected it to happen, but as the competition went on we did start to dream a bit. The victory over AC Milan in Istanbul was incredible but

I'm sure the manager will want to build on that now rather than dwell on it."

"The other side of the coin is that we let ourselves down in the league last season and we'll need to improve this year. We lost too many games away from home but I'm sure we can put that right now that the manager has been here for a year and understands the Premiership a lot better."

"We really have to move forward in the league now and try to challenge the top three. We've shown we can compete with and beat the best teams in Europe so there's no reason why we can't maintain a level of consistency in the league as well. We need to go a lot closer this year and we're all sure we will."

"To finish only fifth last season was a big disappointment but the league table doesn't lie. We finished where we deserved to finish because over the course of the season we weren't good enough."

"We need to make a good start this season and get ourselves up there from the start. Then we can have something to build on rather than just playing catch-up from an early stage."

Carragher is sure to be a regular member of Rafa's starting eleven again this season – and he hopes that will be the case for many more years to come.

"I don't want to ever leave this club," he said. "Very few players can leave here and go to a bigger club. I want to stay here for the rest of my career, there's no doubt about that."

"We definitely have a bright future ahead of us. The boss is gradually starting to bring in the players he wants and the more time we spend together then the better we'll be."

"The fans haven't had too much to celebrate over recent years but last season was hopefully the start of the big trophies coming back to the club again. That's what we're all aiming for."

JAMIE CARRAGHER

23

PETER CROUCH

Peter was born in Macclesfield on January 30, 1981. He started his career at Tottenham Hotspur but after failing to make an impression at White Hart Lane he moved to Queens Park Rangers in 2000. He then had a spell with Portsmouth and scored 18 goals in 37 appearances. Crouch then had spells with Aston Villa and Norwich City before joining Southampton in 2004.

Crouch stands at a very tall six foot seven and is officially the tallest Liverpool player ever. In a relegated Southampton team Crouch was the Saints leading scorer with 16 goals from 24 starts. Crouch scored against Liverpool in a 2-0 win for Southampton at St Mary's Stadium last season in January 2005. Crouch has six England under-21 caps and one goal. Crouch was then handed his England debut on the summer tour of the USA in May 2005 and set up a goal for Michael Owen against Colombia.

Crouch follows in a long line of players to play for both Southampton and Liverpool. The list includes Bruce Grobbelaar, Kevin Keegan, Mark Wright, Sammy Lee, Jimmy Case, Jimmy Melia, Neil Ruddock, David Speedie, Barry Venison, Mark Walters, Paul Jones and Jamie Redknapp.

INTERVIEW

Peter Crouch has revealed how Jamie Redknapp told him he couldn't turn down the opportunity of joining 'the best club in the world'. The 24 year old striker admits it was an easy decision to sign for the Reds, especially after several glowing reports from a former Liverpool captain.

Crouch said: "I obviously know Jamie very well from Southampton and we spoke a lot about Liverpool. We had a number of chats and he told me I had to go and join the best club in the world.

"He told me all about the club, the facilities, the stadium and the fans. Although his dad is the manager at Southampton, he knew what was best for me. He said the fans here are the best in the country and that I'd love to have them on my side."

"To be honest it wasn't a difficult decision for me to make. As soon as I knew about the interest from Liverpool I was eager to come, just like anyone would. It's a club with a great tradition and with the success last year it is a challenge that I'm really relishing. When Liverpool are interested it's difficult to think about any other team. I know there were a few other teams interested but I had my heart set on coming here."

"I know about Liverpool's history and about the Liverpool supporters and it's an honour to be here."

Crouch is perhaps most famous for his giant 6 foot 7 inches frame – but he insists there is much more to his game than his obvious ability in the air.

"I'm really excited about this move. I think I will bring something different to the team," he said. "I'm obviously tall but I also think I'm decent on the ground as well as in the air. Hopefully I'll get a good run in the side and prove it to the supporters."

"I'm confident I can do well at this level. I know there's a lot of quality players already at the club and competition for places is going to be very fierce, but I have confidence in myself to score goals for Liverpool."

"I know it will be hard to keep a place in the side. You don't expect to come to a club like this and expect not to have to compete with other players. I think there are a lot of good players here and I'm not going to make any bones about it, it will be difficult to break into the side. I am confident that I will do and that when I do I will stay there."

"I'm just desperate to play games and show everyone what I can do. When people do see me play they are often surprised I can play on the floor as well and I'd like to think I can bring that to the team and also be a different option."

BOLO ZENDEN

1. Boudewijn Zenden – better known as 'Bolo' – completed his free transfer move from Middlesbrough to Liverpool on July 3 2005.

2. He was considered the natural successor to Marc Overmars when he burst onto the scene with PSV Eindhoven in the 1994-95 season.

3. He made an instant impact with PSV and helped them to win the Dutch championship the following season.

4. He was named Dutch Player of the Year in 1998 before earning a move to Spanish giants Barcelona.

5. After a three year spell at the Nou Camp he moved to Chelsea for £7.5 million in August 2001.

6. Two years later he joined Middlesbrough on a season long loan and scored the winning penalty in the shoot-out to give Steve McLaren's side victory over Bolton in the Carling Cup final.

7. He has won almost half a century of caps for the Dutch national team and played in Euro 2004.

8. He signed a permanent deal with Middlesbrough in the summer of 2004 following his successful loan spell at the Riverside Stadium.

9. He scored against Liverpool for 'Boro during a 2-0 home victory over the Reds in the Premiership last season.

10. He can play either in the centre or on the left of midfield and was Rafa Benitez's first signing after the Reds celebrated their Champions League success

PEPE REINA

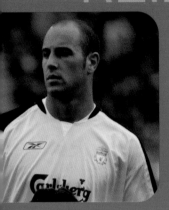

INTERVIEW

New goalkeeper Jose 'Pepe' Reina has revealed how a chat with fellow Spaniard Xabi Alonso convinced him to turn down other Premiership clubs in preference for a move to Liverpool.

As soon as Reina decided to bring his career with Villareal to an end he admits there were several persuasive factors which contributed in his decision to join Rafael Benitez on Merseyside.

"I'm quite close to Xabi," he said. "We became good friends in the national side."

"I was asking him loads of things about the place and he was telling me everything about it and it was all really positive."

"It made me really keen to come here - I was dying to come here in fact - and it's all true what he said about the place."

If Reina is convinced he made the right move then that view is shared by his manager who is delighted to have secured the services of the best young goalkeeper in Spain.

Benitez said: "He has been in the national team and he is a very good boy.

"He likes football, he is a good worker, he is very positive and his attitude is very good."

"He has the quality as a person, as a professional and as a player that in my opinion is what a player needs. For me, he is the best young goalkeeper in Spanish football."

He may be playing second fiddle to Iker Casillas at national level at the present time, but Reina is hoping a move to the European Champions can ultimately be rewarded by full recognition for his country.

"I think whichever team you play for you get noticed - it doesn't matter whether it's here or in Spain," he said.

"There is a rivalry between Casillas and myself but it's purely on a sporting level, there's no problem between us and the most important thing is we're fighting for the team and for Spain."

"The manager did wish me all the best and told me he would be keeping an eye on me from afar and that it won't make any difference whether I'm playing here or in Spain."

He added: I am grateful for any comments the Liverpool manager has said about me but I think now is the time for me to prove it and not just talk about it.

"I know nothing is given on a plate or taken for granted here and I know I will have to fight hard for my place and try to convince the manager to put me in. There is tough competition here at Liverpool and I want to earn my place."

"The manager is aware of what I can do as he has seen me for a number of years in Spain. It was a big influence his presence here but more than anything it is the history and the greatness of the past at Liverpool that has impressed me."

"I am loving every second of this new adventure in my life and I am confident I can be successful with this great club. It's an honour to be part of the Liverpool squad and I intend to make the most of the opportunity which has come my way."

MOMO SISSOKO

Mali international Momo Sissoko accepts he might not be the most popular footballer across the whole of Merseyside this season.

The highly rated Mali international became another of Rafael Benitez's summer signings when he arrived from Valencia in July.

Benitez admits he only realised the tough tackling midfielder was available for transfer when he read in a daily newspaper that he was close to agreeing a move to Everton.

Liverpool stepped in quickly to register their interest and Sissoko admits he had no hesitation in turning the Blues down and teaming up once again with Benitez at Anfield.

"I understand that the Everton fans are angry but I am going to be happier at Liverpool," said Sissoko. "I'm sure they will give me a hard time in the derby match."

"I appreciated the Everton offer, they talked to Valencia and then to me but I was not convinced about everything."

"And when Rafa Benitez appeared, it made my mind up. I could never turn this offer down. If Rafa was not Liverpool boss it might have been different."

"He knows me well and that counts for a lot. I will give 200 percent to carry out his orders on the pitch."

Sissoko already has a lot to live up to after Benitez declared he could be an even better player than former Arsenal star Patrick Vieira.

"He's a young central midfielder who plays a high energy game with a high tempo," said the manager. "He's young, he's not bad on the ball and he will improve the balance of our team."

"He's had two good years with Valencia where he has won trophies. I know him well and he's a very good player."

"I've said many times that he could be as good as Patrick Vieira given time – maybe even better!"

So what does Sissoko make of this favourable comparison? ""I'm not annoyed, I'm flattered," he responded. "I don't think it puts any extra pressure on my shoulders.

"I'm well aware of the English game, I've watched many matches involving Arsenal, Manchester United, Liverpool and Chelsea. Yes, there are different styles but I'm not frightened of it."

"The big difference is that in England players give 200 per cent all the time. I'm a strong player and my playing style is that I run my socks off for the shirt I'm playing in. A lot of people have confidence in me and I'm ambitious to prove them right. When I signed for Liverpool, people were ecstatic back in Mali."

"We have a great squad here full of quality players and I know we can be successful. The squad is strong, the manager is one of the best and I know all about the supporters and the passion they have for the club. I am looking forward to being successful here."

1. Luis was born in Badalona, Spain, on June 24th 1978.

2. He came up through the youth ranks at FC Barcelona and spent two seasons as a regular in the reserves team from 1997 to 1999.

3. He played for Rafael Benitez at Tenerife where he made a vital contribution to their promotion campaign, playing 40 games and scoring 16 goals.

4. After spells with Valladolid and Atletico Madrid in 2002 he returned to FC Barcelona in 2003.

5. He completed his transfer to Liverpool in August 2004.

6. Despite not speaking a word of his new language on the day he moved to Merseyside, the Spaniard was able to conduct interviews in English by the end of the season.

7. He contributed five goals to Liverpool's glorious Champions League campaign, including crucial strikes against Bayer Leverkusen, Juventus and Chelsea in the knock-out stages.

8. Such were the level of Garcia's performances during his debut season on Merseyside that Finnish star Sami Hyypia labelled him 'the new Litmanen'.

9. He says his goalscoring celebration of sucking his thumb after hitting the back of the net is a dedication to his young baby boy.

10. He made his full debut for Spain in a friendly match with China in March 2005.

LUIS GARCIA

10

PHIL NEAL HOLDS THE RECORD FOR MOST CONSECUTIVE APPEARANCES FOR

1. He was born in Smithfield, Australia on September 22 1978.

2. Harry turned down the opportunity of signing for Manchester United to live out his boyhood dream and join Liverpool.

3. He took over the famous Anfield number seven shirt when he arrived, worn by such legends as Kevin Keegan and Kenny Dalglish.

4. Harry started his footballing life at the New South Wales Football Academy in Australia in August 1994 before he was spotted by then Leeds manager Howard Wilkinson.

5. He made his professional debut at the age of 17 when he appeared as a substitute for Leeds against Middlesbrough.

6. His first goal for Liverpool came in the Merseyside derby at Goodison Park in September 2003.

7. He netted eleven goals in an impressive first season at Anfield.

8. In February 2004 he was named Oceania Player of the Year.

9. He has promised that he intends returning to his best form this season having put an injury ravaged year behind him.

10. He played a part in Liverpool's Champions League final success, although he was forced to leave the field in the first half with an injury.

HARRY KEWELL

7

1. Fernando was the top scorer in the Champions League when playing for Monaco during season 2003-04.

2. He scored twice on his international debut for Spain against Sweden back in 1998.

3. Fernando began his playing career with Real Zaragoza, where he scored 28 goals in 66 games.

4. He scored in the Champions League final for Real Madrid against Valencia in their 3-0 win in 2001.

5. His two all-time sporting heroes are former Olympic Gold Medallist Carl Lewis and Miguel Indurain, Spain's greatest ever cyclist, who won five consecutive Tour De France competitions.

6. He managed three goals for the Reds last season, netting his first in a crucial away win at Charlton.

7. His first Anfield goal came with a fine glancing header against Fulham on February 5.

8. Despite Spain disappointing during Euro 2004, Morientes did hit the back of the net for his country in the competition.

9. Fernando watched the Champions League final from the press box in Istanbul where he was working for the Spanish media - and he was celebrating as wildly as any Liverpool fan at the end.

10. While fellow countryman Antonio Nunez has a law degree, Fernando specialised in computer studies and management at school. He admits to surfing the web almost to every day and enjoys playing football computer games.

FERNANDO MORIENTES

19

1. Milan was the tournament's top goalscorer for the Czech Republic during Euro 2004.

2. He carried his good goalscoring form into last season as well and ended joint top scorer with Luis Garcia and Steven Gerrard with 13 goals.

3. Baros signed for Liverpool on the same day as french striker, Nicolas Anelka.

4. He scored two goals on his Premiership debut for Liverpool – away at Bolton Wanderers.

5. He was nicknamed the 'Ostravan Maradona' in his homeland where his impressive form for Banik Ostrava earned him international recognition – and ultimately a move to the Premiership.

6. His Liverpool debut arrived in the Champions League against Barcelona in March 2002.

7. He became the club's third Czech player when he arrived, following in the footsteps of Patrik Berger and Vladimir Smicer.

8. He missed six months of the 2003-04 season after breaking his ankle at Blackburn Rovers.

9. Liverpool initially had a work permit application for Baros rejected, but they were successful on appeal and able to bring him to English football.

10. Only four players appeared in more games for the Reds last season.

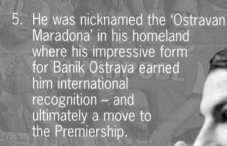

5 MILAN BAROS

P15
Champions League Quiz 2004-05

1. Graz AK
2. Monaco, Olympiacos, Deportivo La Coruna
3. Djibril Cisse
4. 2
5. Neil Mellor
6. Luis Garcia
7. 6-2
8. Sami Hyypia
9. Eidur Gudjohnsen
10. 3-2

P18
Knowledge Quiz Part 1

1. Malaga
2. Barcelona
3. AS Roma (pre-season game)
4. Chelsea
5. Coventry City
6. Fulham
7. Monaco
8. West Bromwich
9. Danny Murphy
10. Pako Ayesteran
11. Tottenham
12. Bolton

P26
Knowledge Quiz Part 2

13. Roy Evans
14. Michael Robinson
15. West Bromwich
16. Five
17. Alan Kennedy
18. Valencia
19. Real Madrid
20. Madrid
21. Emlyn Hughes
22. Valencia
23. 7
24. Didi Hamann, Djibril Cisse and Vladimir Smicer

P32
Liverpool by numbers Quiz

1. 5
2. 1990
3. 61,905
4. 23
5. 17
6. 52
7. 40
8. 3
9. 1892
10. 1928

P37
Photo Quiz

1	2	3	4	5
Xabi Alonso	Jamie Carragher	Djibril Cisse	Jerzy Dudek	Luis Garcia

6	7	8	9	10
Steven Gerrard	Dietmar Hamann	Sami Hyypia	Harry Kewell	John Arne Riise